Teacher's notes
for Guided Reading

THE RAILWAY CHILDREN

Teacher's notes by Alison Kelly
Roehampton University
and Suzanne Maile
Sheen Mount School

Contents

Essential information

National Curriculum level: 3B

Genre: family story

Word count: 2,379

High frequency words

a	about	after	again	all	an
and	are	as	at	away	back
be	because	bed	been	blue	boy
brother	brown	but	by	call(ed)	came
can	can't	cat	come	could	day
did	do	don't	dig(ging)	door	down
first	for	from	get	girl	go
going	good	got	had	half	has
have	he	help	her	here	him
his	home	house	how	I	if
in	is	it	jump	just	last
like	little	live	look	love	made
make	man	may	me	more	much
must	my	name	new	next	night
no	not	now	of	off	old
on	once	one	or	our	out
over	people	play	pull(ed)	put	red
said	saw	see	seen	she	sister
so	some	take	than	that	the

(continued over the page)

High frequency words (continued)

their	them	then	there	they	this
three	time	to	too	tree	two
up	us	very	want	was	water
way	we	went	were	what	when
where	white	who	will	with	would
yes	you	your			

Interest words and phrases

Government	shawl	apology accepted
deafening roar	implored	landslide
heroes and heroines	bunting	accused

Background

Some children may already know E. Nesbit's famous story of a comfortable middle-class Edwardian family forced to leave their prosperous London life by the false accusation and imprisonment of their father. Their relocation to a house in the country near a railway line leads to unexpected adventures, and the eventual release of their father. In this adaptation, the full flavour of the children's characters and lifestyle has been retained, and Alan Marks' atmospheric illustrations do a fine job in evoking the ups and downs of their lives in the country.

Introducing the story

Before you start the reading session or sessions, spend a little time preparing with your group.
You might like to collect some pictures beforehand of the different forms of transport that were available in the 1900s.

Find out if any of the children know the book already – maybe through the film version or a television adaptation. For those who do not know it, start by saying the story is about a family who lived 100 years ago.

You might ask:
- What do you know about those times?
- Did people wear the same clothes, live in the same kind of houses, speak the same way and play the same games?

Make a list of ideas.

Look at the front cover and ask the children what that tells them about the period. Look at your transport pictures together, reminding them that very few people had cars and that trains were steam-driven.

(continued over the page)

Share learning objectives with your group.

The children are going to learn or practise the following:

- understanding how dialogue is used in characterisation
- observing how language changes over time
- noting how descriptive language can be used effectively.

You might say:

- We are going to look at how conversations can tell us what people are like
- We are going to look at how people many years ago spoke differently from the present day
- We are going to look at how well language can be used for describing things.

Turn to the back page and read the biography of E. Nesbit. You could explain that she is one of the first authors to make children the heroes and heroines in stories. She wrote as "E" rather than "Edith" because she didn't want people to think her books were only for girls.

Now go on to the Walkthrough (see next page).

Walkthrough

The walkthrough allows you to "warm" the text for the children by taking them through it without actually reading it.

- You might use it to identify key vocabulary, language patterns and concepts that children could need support with
- You can identify phoneme-grapheme relationships that are to be practised
- It can be a way to identify key "thinking points" in the story (for example, where predictions might be made, characters' thoughts inferred and so on).

Using a copy of the book, look through it with the children. We have suggested pause points and prompts.

Talk through pages 3-5
and make sure the
children note the names
of the characters and
their relationships.

You might ask:
- How do the family live?
- Are they rich or poor?
- How can you tell?

Chapter 1

Change

It all began at Peter's birthday
party. The servants were just
bringing out the birthday cake,
when the doorbell clanged sharply.

3

"Bother!" exclaimed Father.
"Who can that be? Start without me
everyone. I'll be back in a minute."
    Peering into the hallway, Peter
saw Father leading two men into
his study.
    "Who are they, Mother?" asked
his sister, Phyllis.

"I don't know," said
Mother, frowning.
"Stay here. I'm going
to find out."

Mother disappeared into the
study for ages.
    "What's going on?" asked Phyllis.
    "We'll just have to wait and see,"
replied Bobbie, the eldest.

5

Point out that Bobbie is a girl.
- What do you think her real name might be?
  (Roberta)

Go on to pages 6-7.

Mother emerged just as the front door slammed shut. Bobbie saw a carriage and horses driving rapidly away into the night. Mother's face was icy white and her eyes glittered with tears.

"Where's Father?" demanded Peter, running into the empty study.

"He's gone away." Mother was shaking now. Bobbie reached for her hand and held it tight.

"But he hasn't even packed his clothes," said Phyllis.

"He had to go quickly – on business," Mother replied.

Read the sentence describing Mother's emotions, drawing the children's attention to the phrases "icy white" and "glittered with tears".

- Why are these such good descriptions?

"Was it to do with the Government?" asked Peter. Father worked in a Government office.

"Yes. Don't ask me questions, darlings. I can't tell you anything. Please just go to bed."

Upstairs, the children tried endlessly to work out where Father had gone. The next few days were just as strange.

8

All the maids left. Then a FOR SALE sign went up outside the house. The beautiful furniture was sold and meals now consisted of plain, cheap food. Mother was hardly ever at home.

9

"What's happening?" asked Peter, finally. "Please tell us."

"We've got to play at being poor for a bit," Mother replied. "We're going to leave London, and live far away in the countryside."

"Father is going to be away for some time," she went on. "But everything will come right in the end, I promise."

10

Note the language used.

- Discuss how words change over time and how this affects the way we speak.

- Pick out words that are no longer in common use or which reflect the period, e.g. the formal "Father" and "Mother", "carriage and horses".

Go on to pages 12-13, where Bobbie, Peter and Phyllis see a train.

- You could play them a video clip of an old steam train which will help them appreciate the noise the old trains made (you can find one in advance on a railway museum website).

- Note the use of "shriek" and "snort" to describe the train and Peter's use of the word "dragon". Are these effective words?

The next day Bobbie, Peter and Phyllis woke early to explore. They raced outside until they came to a red-brick bridge.

Suddenly there was a shriek and a snort and a train shot out from under it.

"It's exactly like a dragon," Peter shouted above the noise. "Did you feel the hot air from its breath?"

"Perhaps it's going to London," Phyllis yelled.

"Father might still be there," shrieked Bobbie. "If it's a magic dragon, it'll send our love to Father. Let's wave."

Now go on to page 25.

You might ask:

- How have the children's lives changed?

- How do you think they are feeling about living in the country?

- Is their behaviour different now?

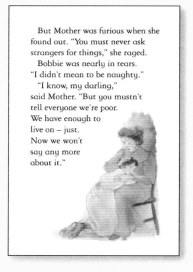

But Mother was furious when she found out. "You must never ask strangers for things," she raged.

Bobbie was nearly in tears. "I didn't mean to be naughty."

"I know, my darling," said Mother. "But you mustn't tell everyone we're poor. We have enough to live on – just. Now we won't say any more about it."

The children should now be ready to read independently. This can be done over several sessions, depending on their experience and ability. We have allowed for three sessions, but you might take more or fewer.

Independent reading and strategy check

Before the children begin reading, include a strategy check to help them tackle difficult or unfamiliar words.

You might say:

· Let's remember what we do when we can't read a word.
  Elicit suggestions from the children, e.g. blend the phonemes, read ahead.

Ask the children to read aloud, a little at a time, either all together or in turns, whilst you listen and monitor. Encourage them to use cues to work out unfamiliar words, and praise fluent reading or good use of strategies.

In each session, encourage reading with expression, noting how the characters would have sounded. Pick out exclamation marks and clues in the language as to how to read the dialogue e.g. "exclaimed", "asked", "demanded". Ask the children to note examples of vivid description as they read.

For assessment purposes, you may want to use the chart on pages 40-41 to note strategies that each child uses, or errors or comments that he or she makes, during the reading.

Ask the children to read chapters 1 and 2 (pages 3-25) whilst you monitor and record strategies.

Chapter 1

Change

It all began at Peter's birthday party. The servants were just bringing out the birthday cake, when the doorbell clanged sharply.

3

"Bother!" exclaimed Father. "Who can that be? Start without me everyone. I'll be back in a minute."

Peering into the hallway, Peter saw Father leading two men into his study.

"Who are they, Mother?" asked his sister, Phyllis.

"I don't know," said Mother, frowning. "Stay here. I'm going to find out."

Mother disappeared into the study for ages.

"What's going on?" asked Phyllis.

"We'll just have to wait and see," replied Bobbie, the eldest.

5

Mother emerged just as the front door slammed shut. Bobbie saw a carriage and horses driving rapidly away into the night. Mother's face was icy white and her eyes glittered with tears.

"Where's Father?" demanded Peter, running into the empty study.

"He's gone away." Mother was shaking now. Bobbie reached for her hand and held it tight.

"But he hasn't even packed his clothes," said Phyllis.

"He had to go quickly – on business," Mother replied.

pages 6-7

"Was it to do with the Government?" asked Peter. Father worked in a Government office.

"Yes. Don't ask me questions, darlings. I can't tell you anything. Please just go to bed."

Upstairs, the children tried endlessly to work out where Father had gone. The next few days were just as strange.

8

Pause after page 8.
Note the word "Government" and the importance of Father's work.

Now ask the children to read on whilst you monitor and record strategies.

All the maids left. Then a FOR SALE sign went up outside the house. The beautiful furniture was sold and meals now consisted of plain, cheap food. Mother was hardly ever at home.

9

"What's happening?" asked Peter, finally. "Please tell us."

"We've got to play at being poor for a bit," Mother replied. "We're going to leave London, and live far away in the countryside."

"Father is going to be away for some time," she went on. "But everything will come right in the end, I promise."

10

Pause after page 10.

- Why did Mother say that they were going to "play at being poor"?
- Why do you think the family have to move?

Discuss the importance of the husband and father in Edwardian times.

Now ask the children to read on whilst you monitor and record strategies.

Chapter 2

A coal thief

After a long, long journey, they arrived at the new house, late at night. Mother rushed around, digging sheets out of suitcases.

The next day Bobbie, Peter and Phyllis woke early to explore. They raced outside until they came to a red-brick bridge.

Suddenly there was a shriek and a snort and a train shot out from under it.

"It's exactly like a dragon," Peter shouted above the noise. "Did you feel the hot air from its breath?"

"Perhaps it's going to London," Phyllis yelled.

"Father might still be there," shrieked Bobbie. "If it's a magic dragon, it'll send our love to Father. Let's wave."

pages 12-13

They pulled out their handkerchiefs and waved them in the breeze. Out of a first class carriage window a hand waved back. It was an old gentleman's hand, holding a newspaper.

After that, the children waved every day, rain or shine, at the old gentleman on the 9:15 train to London.

14

Pause after page 14.

You might want to sound a warning note here about the dangers of playing near railway lines and waving at strangers.

Now ask the children to read on to page 16.

The weather grew colder. Mother sat in her icy bedroom wrapped in shawls, writing stories to earn money for them all.

Bobbie, Peter and Phyllis didn't notice the cold much. They were too busy playing. But one morning, it snowed so much they had to stay inside.

"Please let me light a fire, Mother," begged Bobbie. "We're all freezing."

"Not until tonight, I'm afraid. We can't afford to burn coal all day. Put on more clothes if you're chilly."

Peter was furious. "I'm the man in this family now," he stormed. "And I think we ought to be warm."

Pause after page 16.

- Why did Peter get so cross?

  Note the use of "stormed". Can they read this paragraph with appropriate intonation?

Now ask the children to read on to page 23.

Over the next few days Peter began to disappear without saying where he was going.

"I can't understand it," Mother said soon after. "The coal never seems to run out."

"Let's follow Pete," Bobbie whispered to Phyllis. "I'm sure he's up to something."

17

They trailed him all the way to the station, and watched him pile a cart with coal from a huge heap. Then suddenly, Peter screamed.

A hand had shot out of the darkness and grabbed him by the shoulder.

It was Mr. Perks, the station master. "Don't you know stealing is wrong?" he shouted.

"Wasn't stealing. I was mining for treasure," sulked Peter.

"That treasure belongs to the railway, young man, not you."

20

"He shouldn't have done it, Mr. Perks," said Bobbie, shocked. "But he was only trying to help Mother. He's really sorry, aren't you, Pete?" She gave him a kick and Peter muttered an apology.

"Accepted," said Perks. "But don't do it again."

"I hate being poor," grumbled Peter, kicking the cobbles on their way home. "And Mother deserves better than this."

Soon after, Mother got very sick. Bobbie didn't know how they were going to pay for her medicines, until she had a brilliant idea.

22

She wrote a letter to the old gentleman on the 9:15 train to London and asked Mr. Perks to give it to him.

Dear Mr. (we don't know your name),
    Mother is sick and we can't afford the things the doctor says she needs.
This is the list:
        Medicine   Port Wine
        Fruit   Soda water
    I don't know who else to ask. Father will pay you back when he comes home, or I will when I grow up.
                    Bobbie

P.S. Please give them to Mr. Perks, the station master, and Pete will fetch them

Pause after page 23.

- Look at the letter together, and the items requested.

You might ask:

- Should they have written to a stranger?

Now ask the children to read on to page 25.

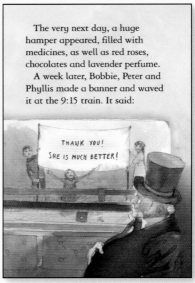

The very next day, a huge hamper appeared, filled with medicines, as well as red roses, chocolates and lavender perfume.

A week later, Bobbie, Peter and Phyllis made a banner and waved it at the 9:15 train. It said:

THANK YOU!
SHE IS MUCH BETTER!

page 24

But Mother was furious when she found out. "You must never ask strangers for things," she raged.

Bobbie was nearly in tears. "I didn't mean to be naughty."

"I know, my darling," said Mother. "But you mustn't tell everyone we're poor. We have enough to live on – just. Now we won't say any more about it."

Pause after page 25.
You might ask:

- Why was Mother angry?

- Why do you think she doesn't want people to know they are poor?

- What kinds of things make your mother angry?

Suggested session 2

If you are reading the story in more than one session,
you might like to go over the story so far. What do
the children remember from the previous session?
Look through the first part of the book to refresh
their memories.

**When you are ready, ask the children to read
chapters 3 and 4** (pages 26-48), whilst you monitor
and record strategies.

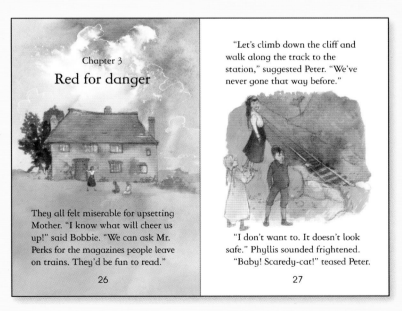

Chapter 3

Red for danger

They all felt miserable for upsetting
Mother. "I know what will cheer us
up!" said Bobbie. "We can ask Mr.
Perks for the magazines people leave
on trains. They'd be fun to read."

26

"Let's climb down the cliff and
walk along the track to the
station," suggested Peter. "We've
never gone that way before."

"I don't want to. It doesn't look
safe." Phyllis sounded frightened.
"Baby! Scaredy-cat!" teased Peter.

27

"It's all right, Phil," Bobbie comforted her. "The cliff isn't that steep."

"Two against one," crowed Peter. "Come on, Phil, you'll enjoy it."

Slowly Phyllis followed her brother and sister, muttering, "I still don't want to..."

28

They scrambled down the cliff. Phyllis tumbled down the last bit where the steps had crumbled away, and tore her dress.

Now her red petticoat flapped through the tear as she walked.

"There!" she announced. "I told you this would be horrible, and it is!"

"No, it isn't," disagreed Peter.

"What's that noise?" asked Bobbie suddenly.

A strange sound, like far off thunder, began and stopped. Then it started again, getting louder and more rumbling.

30

"Look at that tree!" cried Peter. The tree was moving, not like a normal tree when the wind blows, but all in one piece.

All the trees on the bank seemed to be slowly sliding downhill, like a marching army.

31

Suddenly, rocks, trees, grasses, bushes and earth gathered speed in a deafening roar and collapsed in a heap on the railway track.

"I don't like it!" shrieked Phyllis. "It's much too magic for me!"

"It's all coming down," said Peter in a shaky voice. Then he cried out, "Oh!"

The others looked at him.

"The 11:29 train! It'll be along any minute. There'll be a terrible accident."

"Can we run to the station and tell them?" Bobbie began.

"No time. We need to warn the driver somehow. What can we do?"

33

"Our red petticoats!" Bobbie exclaimed. "Red for danger! We'll tear them up and use them as flags."

"We can't rip our clothes!" Phyllis objected. "What will Mother say?"

"She won't mind." Bobbie was undoing her petticoat as she spoke. "Don't you see, Phil, if we don't stop the train in time, people might be killed?"

34

They quickly snapped thin branches off the nearby trees, tore up the petticoats and made them into flags.

"Two each. Wave one in each hand, and stand on the track so the train can see us," Peter directed. "Then jump out of the way."

35

Phyllis was gasping with fright.
"It's dangerous! I don't like it!"
"Think of saving the train,"
Bobbie implored. "That's what
matters most!"

"It's coming," called Peter,
though his voice was instantly
wiped out in a whirlwind of sound.

36

Pause after page 36.
You could ask:
- Was it a good idea to try and stop the train?
- What would you have done? Can you think of a better way?

Now ask the children to read on to page 39.

As the roaring train thundered
nearer and nearer, Bobbie waved
her flags furiously. She was sure it
was no good, that the train would
never see them in time...
"MOVE!" shouted Peter, as the
train's steam surrounded them in
a cloud of white. But Bobbie
couldn't. She had to make it stop.

With a judder and squeal of brakes the train shuddered to a halt and the driver jumped out. "What's going on?"

Peter and Phyllis showed him the landslide. But not Bobbie. She had fainted and lay on the track, white and quiet as a fallen statue, still gripping her petticoat flags.

38

The driver picked her up and put her in one of the first class carriages. Peter and Phyllis were worried, until finally Bobbie began to cry.

"You kids saved lives today," said the driver. "I expect the Railway Company will give you a reward."

"Just like real heroes and heroines," breathed Phyllis.

Pause after page 39.

- The book doesn't tell us about Mother's reaction. You could ask the children what they think she might have said when the children told her about the landslide.

Now ask the children to read pages 40-41.

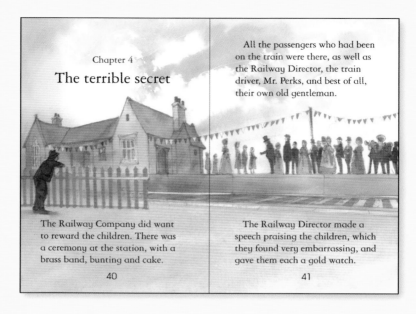

Chapter 4

The terrible secret

All the passengers who had been on the train were there, as well as the Railway Director, the train driver, Mr. Perks, and best of all, their own old gentleman.

The Railway Company did want to reward the children. There was a ceremony at the station, with a brass band, bunting and cake.

40

The Railway Director made a speech praising the children, which they found very embarrassing, and gave them each a gold watch.

41

Pause after page 41.

· Check that the children know what "bunting" is.

You could ask:

· Why do you think the children were embarrassed by the Director's speech?

Now ask the children to read on to page 44.

When it was all over, the old gentleman shook their hands.

"Oh do come back for tea," said Phyllis.

They climbed up the hill together. Bobbie carried the magazines Mr. Perks had collected for her. He'd made a parcel of them, wrapped in an old sheet of newspaper.

42

Back home, Mother, Phyllis and Peter chatted with the old gentleman.

Bobbie went into her room, to sort through the magazines. She undid the newspaper wrapping and idly looked at the print. Then she stared.

Her feet went icy cold and her face burned. When she had read it all, she drew a long, uneven breath.

43

"So now I know," she thought.

It was a report of a spy trial, with a photograph of the accused. It was a photograph of Father. Underneath it said: GUILTY. And then: FIVE YEARS IN JAIL.

Pause after page 44.

You might ask:

- What does Bobbie find out from the newspaper?

- What words can you use to describe her feelings?

Now ask the children to read on to the end of the chapter (page 48).

Bobbie scrunched up the paper. "Oh Daddy," she whispered. "You never did it."

Time passed. The old gentleman left and it grew dark outside. Supper was ready, but Bobbie couldn't join the others.

Mother came to find her. "What's the matter?" she asked.

Bobbie held out the paper. "Tell me about it," she begged.

Mother told her how Father had been arrested for being a spy. Papers had been found in his desk that proved he had sold his country's secrets to enemies.

"Didn't they know he'd never do such a thing?" Bobbie asked.

"There was a man in his office he never quite trusted," Mother replied. "I think he planted those papers on Father."

"Why didn't you tell the lawyers that?" Bobbie wanted to know.

"Do you think I didn't try everything?" Mother demanded. "We just have to be patient and wait for him to come back to us."

"Why didn't you tell us?"

"Are you going to tell the others now you know?"

"No," said Bobbie. "Why?"

pages 46–47

Bobbie thought hard. "Because...
it would only upset them."

"Exactly," said her mother. "But
now you've found out, we must
help each other to be brave."

They went in to supper together,
and though Bobbie's eyes were still
red with tears, Peter and Phyllis
never guessed why.

page 48

Suggested session 3

Go over the story so far. What do the children remember from the previous sessions? Look through the first part of the book to refresh their memories.

When you are ready, ask the children to read Chapter 5 (pages 49-63), whilst you monitor and record strategies.

Mother was unhappy, Father was in prison, and she couldn't do anything to help. So she wrote a letter. And once more it was to the old gentleman.

Dear Friend,

Mother says we are not to ask for things for ourselves, but this isn't just for me.

You see what it says in this paper. It isn't true. Father is not a spy. Could you find out who did it, and then they would let Father out of prison.

Think if it was your Daddy, what would you feel? Please help me.

Love from your good friend,

Bobbie

Pause after page 50.

- Why does Bobbie decide to write the letter to the old man?
- Do you think it is a good letter?

Now ask the children to read on to page 63.

Soon after she sent the letter, Bobbie had her twelfth birthday. Mother gave a bracelet she no longer wore, Peter and Phyllis made a cake, and Mr. Perks brought a bunch of flowers from his garden.

page 51

33

It was very different from her last birthday when she'd had a huge party and lots of presents. This one was happy enough. But Bobbie missed Father so badly, her mind was filled with wanting him.

52

Then, one late summer's day, when the roses were out and the corn was ripening to gold, Bobbie found it impossible to concentrate on her lessons.

"Please, Mother," she begged. "Can I go outside?"

"Do you have a headache?" asked Mother.

53

Bobbie thought. "Not really," she replied. "I just feel in a daze. I'd be more alive in the fresh air, I think."

Mother let her go and Bobbie found herself walking down to the station. She felt as if she were in a dream.

At the station, everyone smiled at her and Mr. Perks shook her hand up and down.

"I saw it in the papers," he grinned. "I'm so pleased. And here comes the 11:54 London train, bang on time."

56

"Saw what in the papers?" Bobbie asked, puzzled, but Mr. Perks had turned away, blowing his whistle.

As the train drew into the station, Bobbie was astonished to see handkerchiefs fluttering from every window.

Only three people got out. An old woman with a basket of squawking hens, the grocer's wife with some brown-paper packages, and the third... "Oh! My Daddy, my Daddy!"
Bobbie's cry pierced the air.

People looked out of the windows to see a tall thin man and a little girl rush up to each other with open arms.

pages 58-59

"I felt something strange was going to happen today," said Bobbie as they walked up the hill, "but I never guessed what."

"Didn't Mother get my letter?" Father asked.

"There weren't any letters this morning," Bobbie replied.

60

"Mother wrote to tell me you'd found out," he said. "You've been wonderful. The old gentleman has too. He helped them catch the real spy. Now, Bobbie, run ahead and tell Mother and Peter and Phyllis I'm home."

He paused in the garden, looking around at the rich summer countryside with the hungry eyes of someone who has seen too little of flowers and trees and the wide blue sky.

Mother, Bobbie, Peter and Phyllis stood in the doorway. Father went down the path to join them.

We won't follow him. In that happy moment, in that happy family, no one else is wanted just now.

pages 62-63

36

At the end of the story, you could say:

- E. Nesbit leaves the family on their own at the end of the book because "no one else is wanted". But can you imagine the family supper that night? What speech bubbles would you give to each character sitting round the table?

Now return to the text (see over the page) to discuss whether the children's answers and predictions were correct, and talk about their approaches.

Return to the text

The return to the text allows you to reinforce teaching points, e.g. checking children's understanding, identifying and reinforcing successful decoding strategies.

Look through the story again to recap on strategies the children have used for decoding unfamiliar words (e.g. phonic, graphic, context or syntax).

You might say:
* I really liked the way (*child's name*) worked out how to read (*word or phrase*) – can you tell us how you did it?

Talk about the story as a whole.

You might ask:
* Were there any parts of the story that surprised you?
* Which part (or character or scene) did you like best?
* Did you like the ending? Can you think of a different way the story could have ended?
* Do you know any other stories like this?

Further reading

The Railway Children is in **Series Two** of the **Usborne Young Reading** series, which includes two other adaptations of E. Nesbit, **The Enchanted Castle** and **The Magical Book**. These are some of the titles in Series Two.

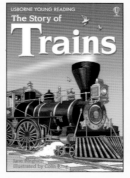

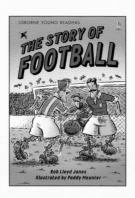

There are over 100 titles available in the Young Reading series, and more are being added all the time. To find out about all the titles available, go to **www.usborne.com**

Guided Reading Record

Text: *The Railway Children –*
National Curriculum Level 3B

Class:...

Group:..

Date:..

Teacher/
Teaching Assistant:...

At Level 3B, it is expected that children:

1. Are gaining independence in using a range of strategies to understand content and meaning.

2. Are beginning to use inference and deduction.

3. Express preferences about characters in books.

4. Are able to discuss alternative meanings of words.

5. Recognise and comment on differences in genres.

6. Are gaining independence in using non-fiction books.

7. Use non-fiction sources to answer questions which have been given by the teacher.

Name:	Name:
Comments:	Comments:
Target:	Target:
Name:	Name:
Comments:	Comments:
Target:	Target:
Name:	Name:
Comments:	Comments:
Target:	Target:

About the Usborne Reading Programme

The Usborne Reading Programme is a collection of over 150 titles for beginner readers, graded in seven levels from very beginners to fully confident readers. Launched in 2002, it has since sold over 6 million copies worldwide.

The Usborne Reading Programme combines vivid, engaging writing with captivating full-colour illustration on every page. From classic tales to lively non-fiction, there is something to appeal to everyone.

From one level to the next, there is a clear progression in terms of subject, style, narrative length, sentence structure and vocabulary, giving children the satisfaction of mastering real books and making measurable progress without overstretching them and causing them to lose enthusiasm.

Non-fiction titles at all levels draw on the expertise of a range of specialists in their subject, ensuring that the books are not only engaging but authoritative: for example, Eva Schloss, stepsister of Anne Frank, advised on **Anne Frank**, and John Woolley of the Captain Cook Memorial Museum in Whitby advised on **Captain Cook**.

The Reading Programme advisers

The Reading Programme has been developed in consultation with **Alison Kelly**, a leading expert in the teaching of reading, who helped to draw up the seven-level framework (see pages 46-47). Alison worked for many years as a primary school teacher in London, and is currently a Senior Lecturer in Education at Roehampton University, teaching about all aspects of literacy.

Suzanne Maile is assistant headteacher at Sheen Mount Primary School in south-west London, a thriving school with a reputation for outstanding teaching and learning. Suzanne is responsible for curriculum development and initial teacher training at Sheen Mount, and has extensive experience in teaching guided reading at all levels. She is also a teacher tutor at Roehampton University, and a consultant teacher for Richmond LEA.

Together, Suzanne and Alison have chosen a selection of titles from the Reading Programme that are particularly suitable for guided reading, and produced comprehensive teacher's notes, packed with ideas and guidance for guided reading sessions.

The range of titles in the Reading Programme provides wide scope for further reading at every level.

The Usborne Reading Programme and the National Curriculum

The Usborne Reading Progamme is fully integrated with the National Curriculum for English at Key Stages 1 and 2, encouraging children to develop fluent and accurate reading across a range of texts, subjects and styles.

Selected titles from all levels of the Reading Programme are available as Guided Reading packs, comprising six copies of the book plus comprehensive teacher's notes. Guided Reading packs represent a selection of text types, and are carefully graded within levels 1-4 of the National Curriculum.

Text type:
European folktale
NC level: 1C

Text type:
Asian folktale
NC level: 1B

Text type: adapted
children's classic
NC level: 1A

Text type:
original fiction
NC level: 2C

Text type:
original fiction
NC level: 2B

Text type:
classic fairytale
NC level: 2A

Text type:
myths and legends
NC level: 3C

Text type: adapted
children's classic
NC level: 3B

Text type:
adapted classic
NC level: 3A

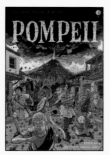

Text type:
non-fiction (history)
NC level: 4C

Text type:
biography
NC level: 4B

Text type:
adapted classic
NC level: 4A

The Usborne Reading

	Number of words	Themes
First Reading Level One National Curriculum level 1	up to 150	Classic tales (e.g. Aesop's Fables and folktales
First Reading Level Two National Curriculum level 1	up to 250	As Level One, including less familiar folktales
First Reading Level Three National Curriculum level 1-2	up to 450	As Level Two plus original fiction and non-fiction (natura history life cycles)
First Reading Level Four National Curriculum level 2	up to 750	As Level Three plus classic fairy tales
Young Reading Series One National Curriculum level 2-3	1,000-1,500	Fairy tales, fantasy fiction, non-fiction ("the story of...")
Young Reading Series Two National Curriculum level 3	2,000-2,500	As Series One plus adapted classics
Young Reading Series Three National Curriculum level 3-4	4,000-5,000	History, biographies classics

The elements above are intended as guidelines only, a
whilst distinctions between different levels remain cle

Programme framework

Content	Vocabulary
Short single narrative followed by reading and comprehension puzzles	Simple everyday vocabulary, familiar items
Single narrative plus character sheets and/or maps, and puzzles	More descriptive and evocative vocabulary, always clear in context
Single narrative with repeated elements, plus character sheets and/or maps, no puzzles	Powerful verbs and adjectives, clear in context
Single narrative	More exotic elements and controlled use of idiom
Several linked stories or one longer narrative in chapters. Direct and indirect speech, intertextual references	Wide-ranging everyday vocabulary
Single narrative in chapters. Introduce irony and subplot, allow opportunity for inference and deduction	More challenging, building on Series One; specialist or technical terms explained
Single narrative in chapters. Assumes some relevant background knowledge	Building on Series Two, may assume knowledge of specialist or technical terms

Exceptions may sometimes be made to individual specifications in the interests of narrative or style.

Edited by Mairi Mackinnon
Designed by Katarina Dragoslavic

First published in 2008 by Usborne Publishing Ltd.,
83-85 Saffron Hill, London ECIN 8RT, England. www.usborne.com
Copyright © 2008 Usborne Publishing Ltd.